A Wild Ride

by Riley Wiseman
illustrated by Coleman Phipps

Practice Decodable 15

McGraw Hill Education

Bothell, WA • Chicago, IL • Columbus, OH • New York, NY

MHEonline.com

Send all inquiries to:
McGraw-Hill Education
8787 Orion Place
Columbus, OH 43240

ISBN: 978-0-02-145055-8
MHID: 0-02-145055-2

Printed in the United States of America.

8 9 10 CTM 23

Miles and Ike stand in a big line.

They get on a ride at nine.

A ride takes Ike and Miles up.

They slide side to side.

They dive down, down, down!

Miles and Ike like to ride!